Gottfried Benn

The Voice Behind the Screen

Translated with
an Introduction by

Simona Draghici

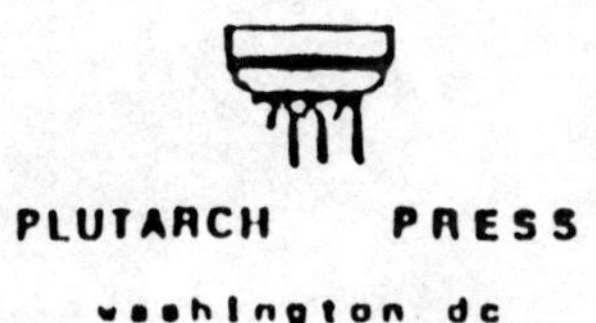

PLUTARCH PRESS

washington dc

This translation first published in the United States of
America by Plutarch Press, Washington, D.C., in 1995.

Complete English translation of GOTTFRIED BENN: DIE STIMME
HINTER DEM VORHANG. Copyright 1952 by Limes Verlag,
Wiesbaden. English translation, Introduction, Chronology
and Notes © copyright 1996 by Plutarch Press.

For information, address the publisher:
PLUTARCH PRESS
P.O. Box 39012, Washington, D.C., 20016-9012

LIBRARY OF CONGRESS CATALOGING-IN-PUBLICATION DATA:

Benn, Gottfried, 1886-1956.

    (Die Stimme hinter dem Vorhang. English)
    The Voice Behind the Screen / Gottfried Benn; translated
with and introduction by Simona Draghici.
            p.   cm.
    Includes bibliographical references.
    ISBN 0-943045-10-X (pbk.)
    I. Draghici, Simona, 1937-   . II. Title.
PT2603.E46S713   1966   96-14104
832'.912--dc20   CIP

Manufactured in the United States of America.
Book design and cover by JAY.
Back cover: DR. BENN'S CAFÉ by George Grosz.

CONTENTS

INTRODUCTION

The literary historians call THE VOICE BEHIND THE SCREEN a radio-play, which is the conventional translation of "Hörspiel". It does indeed display some of the features characteristic of the genre, such as, for instance, a succession of lyric epic stations (in the sense of the stations of the cross in the Roman catholic religious cult, for example) that had also been the core formula of the medieval morality plays; it is spoken and not acted; it includes song, and the satirical vein is ever present; the author plays with words and does away with time and space, or rather, manipulates them in such a way as to obtain not only the effect of caricature but also the sense of the eternal and the infinite, inherent in the morality plays. Nevertheless, Benn's play has no action and so no rapidly moving scenes. Instead, it contains existential ruminations, interspersed with anticlimatic remarks that not only contribute to the shift of tension, but also make up for the lack of events. Gottfried Benn, I suspect, was willing to give us in this last play of his (he died four years later of cancer of the spine) something approximating a "Hörspiel" in the literal sense of the term, rather than another specimen of the genre. What he presented us with resembles more a game played not with cards but with loudly uttered words; the attention the participants in the game pay to each other's utterances and train of thought is often problematic and always intermittent. As a literary genre, the radio-play has allegedly come into the world under the impact of the technological development of radio-broadcasting. I doubt, though, that this was also the determining factor in Benn's choice of the work translated here. Rather, the source and the determining medium too seem to have been a combination of his own poetic strain and the coffee-house, with its motley of patrons, snippets of dialogue and truncated conversation. A habitué himself, Benn the poet had often taken solace in the coffee-houses of Berlin, both before and after World

War II. It was also his experience of such public places that led him to the conclusion that a devastation as sweeping as that through which Berlin had gone in the last years of WWII did nothing to change the old habits of its surviving inhabitants. Hence Benn's despair of human self-redemption, which in the play is carefully wrapped in sarcasm with tinges of cynicism. In order to broaden the scope of this conversation piece (a better description, in my opinion, of the play), and subsequently to render its message universal, Benn introduces two additional devices: one, quite ingenious, is the Sunday newspaper with its contents (the real protagonist of Part Two of the play), and the other, the chorus with its leader from the ancient Greek theatre, which takes most of the third and last part of the play.

As one may easily infer from the general title of the work, its world is divided into the here and now, and the beyond; the messages from there to here are transmitted by the ringing of handbells. The beyond, on the other side of the screen, is assigned to the Procreator, addressed by his offspring as Great Father. Although quite inscrutable, the bearded father is not a god-figure in the Judeo-Christian tradition (Benn even makes him rebuke his brood when attempting to mention God by name in one of their repartees): after all, it was people like them who had killed the latter. Benn gives us to understand that he is no deus absconditus, while the screen may be considered to represent the limitations of those sitting on either side of it, the gap between generations, as well as between the dead and the living, rather than the impenetrability of a god-like figure, for instance: children are aliens, the side effect of other pursuits, mainly hedonistic. The Procreator is not impervious to their arguments: his irritation at their insistence attests it, but he resents their expectations which he regards merely as signs of helplessness before life. He resents their persistent need of guidance through it. After all, he is no better, that is to say more knowledgeable than they, only older, and to that one may add, more of a poet at heart: in his own prime, the Procreator had been attracted more by the transfiguration which love was working in his female partners than anything else. When old age took over, his hedonism found another object in nature with its variety of landscapes. On the here and now side of the screen, one listens to the procession of

the brood, ten of them, taking the floor and addressing their procreator in alphabetical order. Alfred, who has also arranged the setting, is the first to speak, but the next in order, Berthold, is late as he keeps looking for what he could say to his father, so Alfred introduces his sister, the third in the row, instead. Her name is Cilly. Eventually, Berthold shows up, and after him Donath. Their existential arguments are illustrated by "concrete" examples. In the first part of Benn's play, also entitled "The Examples", there are four, yet none personifies any of the cardinal sins as they would appear in a morality play. Not only are they more complex but also free of the moralistic aspect characteristic of the medieval genre. Example I is an old lecher, while Example II is the retired civil servant who resignedly tries to kill what time is still left to him in the best ways he knows and the welfare system allows him to. From time to time, he asks himself about the ways of the world, particularly while sitting out on a bench, on any sunny day. To anticipate, it may be said that he is Benn's only positive character, saved in his author's eyes by his resignation to his own lot and his benign sense of humour. Example III is a procuress who has transformed her three-room flat into a brothel and is defending her interests with all the astuteness she is capable of, against the authorities and the moralists. Example IV is a tenement owner and speculator, representing all the ruthlessness of predatory capitalism.
While the first part by and large deals with human intercourse on a local level, so to speak, one can easily imagine its atmosphere to be that of the West Berlin after the Soviet blocade, when the economic recovery in Western Germany was putting out its first shoots, the second, entitled "The Sunday Newspaper", opens a window to the larger world: it is a device that supplies the illusion of the dream come true by bringing the distant and the inaccessible onto everybody's threshold through the Sunday paper (which at the time had not yet yielded to the onslaught of coloured television). It is Emil who brings it in and who is a modern, post WWII poet of sorts, drawing his inspiration from newsprint and versifying the sensational stories in it that appeal to him most. He is joined by Ferdinand, though both are rebuked by Gerhard who sees in the descriptions of distant and exotic lands featured in the newspaper as many sterile incitements to

evasion, to day-dreaming. (It took the West Germans a little longer to become the invasive, mass tourists of those remote regions. Nevertheless, the longing for distant, inaccessible places cannot be uprooted: it is only its object that changes with the increasing accessibility of what once were consider-ed far-away places. The dope persists whether as virtual reality or interplanetary incursions.) In his turn, Gerhard thinks that he has found a solution to his existential crisis by training himself to become an automaton the main quality of which is randomly to register everything that surrounds him. To illustrate his point, he produces Example V, the radar-thinker. The latter is a parody of an earlier portrait Benn had drawn of modern man, sensitive to all outer signals, yet incapable of original thinking with its selective and sustained concentration. Example V differs from any radar installation at work only through his ability to use articu-late language. Then, one after the other, Herwarth, Isaac and Katya join in, giving their opinions on life as they live it and see it lived. At last the Voice (that is to say, the Pro-creator) loses his temper as he grows fed up with the whining and the promiscuous existence described by his brood, throws the bells away and gives his children a last piece of advice in the form of an oracle: 'in darkness we live, in darkness we do what we can.' As for himself, his intentions are to spend the rest of his time sitting in a garden and admiring its changing landscape, and nothing else.
The play's third and last part is entitled "Melancholy and Neon Lights". It comes after the rift between parent and grown-up children, which after all brings to an end the discovery that took most of the first two parts. The third brings back Examples I, II, III and IV, though this time as universals, motive forces behind post WWII human existence. That is exactly what the chorus points to in their brief comments. The whole is rounded off by the chorus leader's dithyramb that addresses the entire continent, nay, more: all that still could be called the Western civilization with its seldom admitted loss of faith in redemption and implicitly in an ultimate authority that would define for each individual his or her place in the universe, the direction of his or her life and a hierarchy of values acceptable to every-body. To the overwhelming incertitude that pervades the universe of human relations, Benn, through the chorus leader,

opposes the creative drive in the individual, who finds salvation by giving expression to that inner creativity. In that way, the chorus leader conveys Benn's own existential direction, pursued in full awareness of the imminent end and of the individual's smallness, his insignificance in the ever-renewed macrocosm.

Such circumstances as those set forth by Gottfried Benn in the play are not conducive to the tragic, either as a dramatic form or as an inherent existential feature. There is nothing noble about the progeniture and their examples: they all are rather dull and predictable in their linear or static existence. They are not possessed by any sense of boundary or limitation, and have no notion of, and so belief in superior forces or a fate that challenge them or they challenge, and as a consequence, they experience no ordeal. Instead, they show a stubborn will to live: they keep going and doing what habit, routine and self-indulgence compel them to, without paying too much attention to the enveloping cosmos, and ignoring deity altogether. Benn distinguishes three main drives in the will to live of his contemporaries: one is the sense of acquisition, another is the pursuit of well-being, and the third is eroticism, love under every form. The questions that Benn's characters ask most often refer to the next moment in their existence and the direction the latter might take: 'what then?' and 'whereto?' Actually, they are never answered, which leaves one with the lived moment, or more accurately, with the experience of the gobbled moment. Even the Procreator wants nothing but to spend his last moments contemplating nature and its seasonal changes: it is not a communion with it, no contemplation of deity through its creation, but mere esthetical perception, a sublimation of his earlier eroticism.

Nonetheless, alongside all those drives, one also comes across the creative urge, the spirit of renewal, that makes itself manifest here and there, in the shadow of death and disaster, in an unfathomable universe that offers no idea of direction, as well as in the absence of any hope of redemption or salvation. If the notion of tragic is irrelevant to Benn's world, it is the individual courage that keeps creativity alive and gives it expression. Goethe, the well of wisdom, to whom so many intellectuals, disgusted with the Nazi régime, turned to, gave Benn no clue, but rather disconcerted him: Goethe had

directly related courage to chance! The effect it had upon
Benn was to bring him back to earth, so to speak, to immunize
him against absolutes. After all, it is in our awareness of
our limitations that we find our safeguards.

Forty years after it was first published, Benn's play still
has something to tell us, the inhabitants of the Western
hemisphere and in particular, those in Europe: the stoic
and dignified resignation to one's lot, frugality and self-
reliance are moral formulae that could well serve those
who are experiencing a wave of disenchantment, especially
since the alleged collapse of the iron curtain, and which
goes much deeper than the apparent squabble between Westies
and Ossies in the reunited Germany. The publication of an
English translation now is intended to help the Goethean
chance. Thus, an opportunity is hereby offered to rethink
our priorities while letting go of the virtual realities with
which we have been padding our existence on our way to deper-
sonalization and collective destruction.

Finally, the translation as such is dedicated to the young
Lutheran pastor who during his Sunday morning sermon at St.
Jacob's church at Weimar, on the 19th March, 1995, was ex-
plaining the meaning of individual freedom to the handful
of parishioners attending mass. Although I ignore his name,
the quiet earnestness with which he was practising his voca-
tion in circumstances that did not escape him, made me all
of a sudden recall the Procreator's oracle in Benn's play.

Washington, DC, May 1995   SIMONA DRAGHICI

SELECT BIBLIOGRAPHY

BENN, Gottfried: PRIMAL VISION; selected writings. Edited by
    E.B. Ashton. New Directions, New York, 1960.
BENN, Gottfried: PROSE, ESSAYS, POEMS. Edited by Volkmar
    Sander, foreword by E.B. Ashton and introduction by Rein-
    hard Paul Becker. Continuum, New York, 1987.
BENN, Gottfried: POEMS, 1937-1947. German and English. Trans-
    lated with an introduction by Simona Draghici. Plutarch
    Press, Washington DC, 1991.
BENN, Gottfried: SELECTED POEMS. Edited By Friedrich Wilhelm
    Wodtke. Introductions and notes in English. Poems in
    German. Oxford University Press, London, 1970.
BENN, Gottfried: DIE STIMME HINTER DEM VORHANG. Limes Verlag,
    Wiesbaden, 1952.
BENN, Gottfried: GESAMMELTE WERKE in 4 Bänden. Edited by
    Bruno Hillebrand. Fischer Taschenbuch Verlag, Frankfurt/M,
    1989-1994.
BENN, Gottfried: GESAMMELTE WERKE. Edited by Gerhard Schuster
    in cooperation with Dr. Ilse Benn. 5 vols. Klett-Cotta,
    Stuttgart, 1986-   .
BENN, Gottfried: GESAMMELTE WERKE in Zwei Bänden. Edited by
    Dieter Wellershoff. Limes Verlag, Wiesbaden, 1973.
ADAMS, Marion: GOTTFRIED BENN'S CRITIQUE OF SUBSTANCE. Van
    Gorcum & Co., Assen, 1969.
ALTER, Reinhard: GOTTFRIED BENN. THE ARTIST AND POLITICS
    (1910-1934). Herbert Lang, Bern, 1976.
ELIOT, T.S.: THE THREE VOICES OF POETRY. Cambridge Univer-
    sity Press, London, 1953.
MANYONI, Angelika: CONSISTENCY OF PHENOTYPE. A Study of
    Gottfried Benn's Views on Lyric Poetry. Peter Lang, New
    York, 1983.
RITCHIE, J.M.: GOTTFRIED BENN - THE UNRECONSTRUCTED EXPRES-
    SIONIST. Oswald Wolff, London, 1972.

CHRONOLOGY

1886 Born at Mansfeld in West Priegnitz (North-West of Berlin, on the 2nd of May, the eldest son of Gustav Benn, a Protestant pastor, himself son and grandson of pastors, and of Caroline, née Jaquier, a French Swiss who had come to Germany as a governess. Ultimately, Gottfried Benn himself became bilingual and came to regard himself as an expressive embodyment of the Mediterranean and the Northern cultures on which European civilization was held to rest. Soon afterwards, the Benn family moved to the village of Sellin, in the province of Neumark, East of Oder, where he was taught by his father and then, alongside the sons of the local nobleman, by a private tutor hired by the latter. In due course, he was enrolled at Frederich Gymnasium at Frankfurt-upon-the-Oder where he acquired a solid classical education. There, too, he met Alfred Henschke, one of his future literary friends, better known by his pen-name of Klabund.

1903 After graduation from the gymnasium, Benn is admitted at Marburg University where he reads German philology and theology at his father's will, though he himself is attracted by the prospects of a scientific career. A year later, Benn transfers to Berlin University. After another year there, he is admitted at the Kaiser Wilhelm Academy of Military Medicine, a step which releases him from his father's authority and allows him to prepare for a scientific career without imposing additional burdens on the modest income of his father who has seven other children to take care of.

1910 Intern at the Charité Hospital in Berlin. A year later, Benn wins a prize for medicine from Berlin University for a research paper, entitled "The Etiology of Epilepsy in Puberty". The following year, Benn passes his doctoral examination at Berlin University with a *thesis on the incidence of diabetes mellitus in the Army. The same year witnesses the publication of his collection of poems THE MORGUE AND OTHER POEMS. His friendship with poetess Else Lasker-Schüler. His second collection of poems, SONS: NEW POEMS, follows a year later and is dedicated to her. Discharged from active service in the Army for reasons of physical disability. In the Spring of 1912, his mother dies of cancer.*

1914 *Ship-doctor on a boat bound for North America. Sea-sickness cuts short prospects for a career in that profession. Instead, Benn becomes a substitute physician at a T.B. sanatorium in the Fichtelgebirge region, North-East of Bayreuth. An earlier attempt at specialization in psychiatry also ended in failure, as Benn realized his inability to meet the challenges which such a job claimed upon one's psyche. Meets his future wife whom he hastily marries on the 1st of August, the day of his remobilization. He also adopts her son on the same day. Benn takes part in the siege of Antwerp; is awarded the Iron Cross, Second Class, after which is posted at Brussels, in charge of an Army brothel. His first story, BRAINS, is published.*

1915 *His only child, daughter Nele, is born. Publishes his first play, DAY'S MARCH. As military physician, witnesses the execution and signs the death certificate of nurse Edith Clavell, sentenced to capital punishment for spying. His book of poems, FLESH: COLLECTED POEMS, sees the light of print. Returns to Berlin where he sets his own medical practice (he will close it in 1935), and embarks upon a parallel literary career. Five years later, his wife, an actress who is his senior by eight years, dies at Jena, following surgery. Later on, Benn entrusts his daughter Nele to the care of a friend in Denmark. Eventually, Nele will bewill become a Danish journalist. That same year sees the publication of the first edition of Benn's COLLECTED WORKS.*

1924 *Travels throughout Germany, France and Spain and goes on writing. Three years later, his book COLLECTED POEMS is brought out.*

1928 *His COLLECTED PROSE follows. His school-friend Klabund* dies; a year later, another of his friends, actress Lili Breda, commits suicide, and the next year, his step-son dies of T.B. at the age of 18. Radio-dialogue with fellow-poet Oskar Loerke. Writes the text for an oratorio with music by Paul Hindemith, THE PERPETUAL.

1932 Admitted to the Poetry Section the Prussian Academy of the Arts. Publishes his essay, GOETHE AND THE NATURAL SCIENCES. A year later, Benn is provisionally appointed to head the Prussian Academy of the Arts, following the removal of Heinrich Mann. Struck off the medical register as suspected Jew (1st April). Reads the funeral oration for the President of the Academy, the composer Max von Schillings (27th July), but is forbidden to deliver his address on the occasion of the poet Stefan George's death in Italy (4th December). A month later, is appointed Vice-President of the Union of National Writers. Repeatedly attacked by the Nazi media for his alleged intellectualism. His medical practice turns into a liability.

1935 Rejoins the Army as all the other ways of making a living out of his medical profession are denied to him. Benn is appointed Surgeon-Major at the Army Recruitment Centre at Hanover where he meets his future second wife. Military life serves him as sound excuse to resign from the German Academy of Poetry and the Union of National Writers.

1936 His new book of verses, SELECTED POEMS is attacked by the Nazi press. A year later, Benn is posted as Surgeon-Major to the GOC Third Army Corps in Berlin. There, he marries Herta von Wedemeyer who has been his secretary at Hanover. Two months later, Benn is forbidden to write and publish.

1939 WWII. Promoted Chief Medical Officer of the Army GHQ in Berlin. In September 1943, is transferred to Landsberg-upon-the-Warthe, East of the Oder, not far from the village of his childhood. Before leaving Berlin, however, he manages to print a private edition of his most recent poems, secretly, under the title TWENTY-TWO POEMS. "Monologue is included in this collection.

1945 As the Eastern Front collapses, Benn flees back to Berlin, and sends his wife to the countryside for shelter. She commits suicide the day the Soviet Army enter the village on the Elbe, where she has taken refuge.

1946 Forbidden to publish by the Allied Forces, Benn's attempts to print his war-time essays and verses remain unsuccessful. In December, marries Dr. Ilse Kaul, a dentist, who moves her practice into his flat. His most formidable opponents are his former fellow-expressionists, Johannes R. Becher and Alfred Döblin. Two years later, Arche Verlag, a Swiss publishing house, breaks the silence by bringing forth a selection of his underground poems, under the general title STATIC POEMS. Then a publisher of Wiesbaden follows the example, thus relaunching Benn on his public, literary career.

1951 The German Literary Academy of Darmstadt awards him the Büchner Prize, officially acknowledging Benn's post-war literary activity.

1953 Benn is awarded the Cross of the Order of Merit of the Federal Republic of Germany. Lectures widely, talks on the radio, writes about art and the artists in the modern world.

1956 Dies of cancer of the spine at Bad Schlagenbad, on the 7th of July, and five days later is buried at the Neue Waldfriedhof in Berlin-Dahlem.

The Voice Behind the Screen

*Dedicated to my wife, **
a generation younger than I,
who with delicate and nimble hands,
arranges the hours, the steps,
and in vases, the asters.

PART ONE:

THE EXAMPLES

ALFRED

Withdrawn as you are behind your screen, Great Father, it is
better so: one doesn't look you in the face. There you may
puff at your pipe or stroke your beard, and also take a nap
whenever you are getting bored. I, for one, am willing to
talk to a wall: it is the natural listener, after all. Whenever you want to make yourself felt, ring! I've put two
different bells for you, there. The softer means: faster,
not so many details. The louder bell: slow down, be more
introspective. When you ring them both together, it means:
you scour the cosmic sphere, I find nothing nearer home. I
start - O.K.?

I am Alfred, your first-born. You have named us according to
the alphabet. Berthold is not here yet; comes later; doesn't
yet know the text he must deliver, what exactly pushes him
up front, it is all confused. The programme reads:*what the
procreator says to his sons and daughters - today. The years
of procreation span between thirty and sixty years back. The
whole thing will be trimmed a little, for sure; nonetheless,
one must not talk gibberish. Personally, I find myself in the
awkward situation in which I can no longer utter what I
should or could. Thus, from the first, a compromise. Either
the matter keeps revolving by itself, and then one need not
speak out, or it must be knocked off and then I need not be
the one who does it.

If the holy is in everything, we must look for it. If great
commandments are given, we must ask ourselves: what is our
position with regard to them? If calls are sent from far-off
worlds, must we strain ourselves to overhear them? "Must" and
"far-off worlds" - is the tempter speaking already? At the
moment, I am busy examining the falterings in otherwise quite
successful marriages. Faithfulness is such a frightful inner
process that, in general, one can neither learn nor teach it.
For all practical purposes, my maxim is valid: good stage
direction is better than faithfulness. To treat your partner
with consideration and not let him or her notice; no need to
be obsessed with the truth in such situations! But as soon as
one's feelings get the better of oneself -

Hello, here comes Cilly! C as in Chérie, also number three.
Cilly, can a woman love two men?

CILLY

Sure, she can.

ALFRED

But when she truly loves one of them, dissolves in his arms,
is like wax in his hands, can she still love another?

CILLY

Sure, she can.

ALFRED

How does she manage it?

CILLY

One of them may be old, and the other, young; one may be a
god and the other, a mortal. She will always feel frightfully
flattered whenever the god copulates with her, but she will
always go with the other. No man may count on love unless he
heeds certain banalities. Before anything else, he must
always be there; whereas the gods are on so many boards of
directors, only goodness knows them all.

ALFRED

If the holy is in everything, then it should also be in
sensuality.

CILLY

Can't you think in practical terms of a proxy or an empowered
deputy? The word comes from the ancient times of Aphrodite.

THE VOICE

No historicism. Concrete examples.

EXAMPLE I

I am the husband, past sixty, and think of it: in the last
few months, I have grown tired of my wife. Nice person, but
then the complications start. When all comes to an end, one
should crawl into the gutter.* In that way one doesn't fall

any lower. What more can happen to one? Divorce? Delirium?
Puerperal fever*is out of the question, anyhow. Death is such
an infamous thing that whoever describes it as the roundness
of the finale*has got a conductor's stick that's all crooked.

ALFRED

No objections to what the man is saying. Cilly, what do you
think?

CILLY

First of all, let us hear more.

EXAMPLE I

And with what lot have I spent these sixty years? Wander just
once through the streets: what monkey show! The restaurant-
keepers stand in the doorways wishing that the passers-by
were hungry and thirsty; the dentists that the abscesses were
at the root of one's teeth, the shoemaker that the upper-
parts of one's shoes split; the clergy that the holy stand
out distinctly, and the lawyers cry murder - all clamour for
rôles, big ones, stuffed with profits and imitation laurel
leaves by the end of the day. None can say quietly: you all
know me; or as the Tao puts it:*results through living.
Thereby none of them are people that have lifted themselves
from down under, but rather obliging folks, lovers of nature,
they want to go to the Königssee, with its steep, rocky banks.

CILLY

There is something in that.

EXAMPLE I

You have spent the years with their like. Faces, faces.*There,
I see a gentleman coming into the pub; has got a wonderful
muffler, padded gloves, takes them off so carefully, smoothes
them all into shape on the peg, as if wanting to stop the
time. Then he sits down so pleased with himself, that the
moon would obviously hang itself to the trellis for his sake.
The whole, a lump: teeth out, tonsils out, appendix out,
uterus out; marked shape that cuts itself out for prophilac-
tic reasons. And at the next table, how happy the gentleman

is when a friend of the landlady clutches his knee: a con-
firmation of good-breeding. In my opinion, all are thieves
of scrap metal,* dealers in alloys; they go to the toilet,
load the urinals into the rucksacks; liquor down the gullet,
sepsis in the liver, sugar in the ureters - but now, the
righteous man who rounds everything off - good for him -
to a meaningful experience, is he the righteous being? No,
he is only a dullard.

THE VOICE

Wait!

EXAMPLE I

So those creatures that now have faces drag themselves over
here through the parks, into their flats, out on journeys: as
many battle-fronts! Greedy, mangled, gray from bad luck and
the necessities of life; and there you know a face which you
want to be close to, drink with, a single face, a particular
face - mind you - should I have given a wide berth to such a
face? If the holy is in everything -

BERTHOLD

I have already heard the last one. But what was it like once
upon a time when you were talking to your wife? Maybe she is
not as dull as you think -

EXAMPLE I

At first I dreaded but now I miss the excitement of it all.

CILLY

But you see, between us, you too have got a face -

BERTHOLD

Is not the holy but an abstraction accompanied by the bass
sounds of an organ?

THE VOICE

About that, later. Berthold, your examples!

EXAMPLE II

I am retired, on social security: not much, but enough for a
nice idler's life. Whenever it rains in the morning, you can
stay at home. If the sun shines instead, you sit out on the
bench. Old - already; but the others must die first; there
are quite a few left. I must have some merit, or at least,
must have had, as I am so much taken care of - or forgotten
- nowadays one shoves right through the day, a look here, a
glance there, and one asks oneself, now which is man's fate?
To roam as Odysseus, seven years with Calypso,* with Circe
in the hammock, looking Nausicaa in the eyes, or to tread
the polar ice like Nansen, or fifty years in an office, putting up with the rules of the old school: strict observation
of holidays and prompt collection of wages. Yesterday, I per-
mitted myself a pair of shoes with arch-support to be made to
order, not because I could not do without it, but all the fuss
beguiles the time.

EXAMPLE III

I run a salon,* you understand already, not that I am immoral,
but the gentlemen have desires that die hard, and so one has
the hands full making all work out without a hitch; evenings
one truly comes out of the water. During the actual business
hours in the morning - a leap from the office or the delivery
van: please park a little farther! Most of them are homely,
but then there comes one who wants the schoolchild scene,
with rod and cane. Atmosphere, ladies! Some gentlemen want
cultured conversation as an introduction: Meran or something
of that sort. In my opinion, if a woman is smart, then all
that is fine, but if she is not, then the whole game is un-
worthy, as when a fiddler is screeching. My ladies are quite
content to stay with me; it's not often that they mumble: so
many ladders in the stockings. You see, not all the squires
have nimble hands. Four pairs of Perlon stockings a week;
they cannot be written down as advertizing expenses in the
tax returns. Certain gentlemen come early in the morning, at
eight o'clock. It fits smack into their business constella-
tions. So one lives through the ups and downs of commerce and
industry.

EXAMPLE IV

I am the landlord, no offence meant. I happen to have been
running a tenement-house throughout the war and also used to
own quite an ellegant villa with a green lawn and the like,
and then sold the villa quite well. Bloody pack of tenants!
Sitting in the cellar all the time, posting pickets, extin-
guishing the incendiary bombs; but for them, people like us
could have settled in more propitious and wholesome parts
of the country. Yet the cockroaches want hot water; well,
even the subtenant finds it convenient to scour his carcass
by hooking into my electric power line. I had to change three
fuses - - and my week-end house in Düsseldorf? There is a
tattered armchair in the room where I receive the grumblers:
sit down, look out, see how I sacrifice everything for you!
But when they turn insolent, it rains through the ceiling and
so on - get out! He hasn't yet favoured the faint-hearted,
the old God: each evening, in the style of Dehmel* I pray:
give me, give me - a rent increase.

THE VOICE

Quite decent types: all rather dull. The pensioner, the
least; the one with Circe in the hammock. I'll look him up
again.

ALFRED

And the holy is everywhere. One must remember that. All that
has come to be: pyramids, martyrs, cathedrals, preludes are
penetrated by it. How does that rhyme together? Somewhere a
great web must stand the test. For a while, all comes to an
end; and after a while, all is there again. One cannot cease,
nor can one start anew. In winter something is going on
which is unlike what is happening in summer. In summer,
something very impetuous surges through all the cracks,
but less so in winter. Anyhow, we always fumble with a sack
pulled down over our eyes, and grope along, at best.

BERTHOLD

Yet one also knows too little. I've lived fifty years and it
is only now that I learn something about mouse-traps. That
they must be handled differently: for field mice, which are

very sensitive to human scent, you must scald the traps after
each successful use; whereas for the small house mouse and
the big, striped, field mouse, which after all, are domestic
animals, you don't have to. Tremendous lessons lie in that
for man and mouse: observations, comparisons,* measurements
and instincts; a whole world in itself, and it remained
closed to me for so long.

DONATH

The same goes for the inner self. Have you ever felt the
great strength which weak, despised people are capable of?
You have an affair with a waitress, waits on patrons, submis-
sive character; crises begin, splits, ruses, breakdowns.
And all of a sudden you find satisfaction in those unpolished
hands: the table is laid, the cutlery set, glasses placed in
front of you, and a genuine warmth, a current surges, and you
go along.

ALFRED

And to enlarge upon such delicate matters. In 1730, the ca-
mellia was introduced in Japan - what a springtime! A flower
was introduced! Still there is la dame aux camelias whom
everybody knows: sad arias; heart-rending syncopations. Sometimes I bury her name in tropical camellias, in courtship;
one doesn't dare to touch the stem in the pot; all of a sudden, the flower falls with a heavy thud, one hears it: a
dream is over - I break loose, too.

THE VOICE

Mellow, mellower, mellowest. No soft spots!

EXAMPLE I

And talking about myself once more, all squandered away,
all the strength gone, yet once again this face, which I've
mentioned, she closed her eyes, longing to sink: all your
entrails are trembling, enraptured and cosy, and next to you
the warmth, the brightness and the good fortune. You may love
your wife, but when you are with the other, you get carried
away, and when you are alone, you think of neither. One is
as near to you as is your vest, and the other, as your tie,

and it goes without saying that you cannot move about naked.

EXAMPLE III

Perhaps I can be of some service to you, in all humbleness. Tell me your type, the voice of this face, this and that, reddish blonde or salt and pepper, and the neck, the nape of the neck -

EXAMPLE II

There you touch a curious problem. The body is nothing, the soul even less; one of my greatest flames had never heard of Nietsche; and I've got the spade of a brain and dig about. I've observed the most beautiful, the smartest, the most spell-binding women, and never linger by them to the very end. But even the inferior lose their sense in this collection and acquire different weights. So what is the whole? A paroxism? An incident? A chance?

EXAMPLE III

A mishap.

EXAMPLE I

Then there should be formal guarantees against it.

EXAMPLE III

My salon is such an insurance and at reasonable rates.

ALFRED, BERTHOLD, DONATH

Now we want to sing the arias.*

ALFRED

To be once more as in earlier times, irresponsible and ignorant of the end. To feel the flesh: thirst, tenderness, conquest, dissolution - touch the other side in the former - in what? To sit there in the evening, pining in the abyss of the night, he cringes, but the ground is covered with flowers, is whiffing fragrances, brisk and quivering; behind all that, decay, naturally. Then it grows quite dark and once more you know your part, fling down the money and go.

BERTHOLD

Early in the morning*the hydrangeas put their heads out of
the bathroom window, pink heads, an outgoing, mute flower;
it is the red of the dawn in them which greeted me. At times,
a tune would also come out of one of the houses, some of it
quite orgiastic: that was in summer. That such things might
happen seems to me now rather reckless. What others too saw
and will see, later or for the first time and ever again
- should not jump into the eyes of such an incurable wretch.

DONATH

Or it is at the tropics, the air dampens your skin, the
drinks, your clothes. What steam! It always turns my thoughts
to earlier times, to ferns and sedimentary formations. At the
next table, on the other hand, salad platters and Coca Cola
fill your sight - so life fulfills itself and tries to get a
rounded-off picture. Yet one always slips either forwards or
backwards, away from things, at an impersonal distance.
The moment: we cannot stop anything, a glimpse around and
everything runs farther. You love a woman, you are with her,
you love her truly, there is nothing like you two, the world
has disappeared, only the night and the words between you two,
those words, goodness alone knows where they come from, the
first words as in Paradise, the last words which unite as
much as they destroy - I said, there is no world out there,
only you two -, but where the pillow ends, what smites you in
the eye? I am asking you, I am not saying anything -

(Both bells ring)

ALFRED, BERTHOLD, DONATH

But why cosmic? I don't understand.

THE VOICE

Sorry, I had dozed away and dropped both bells.

ALFRED

You look out through a balcony doorway, over the geraniums,
into the night. Now she is fanning herself under your penetrating gaze; overhead, the white nights of Stockholm; they

are dancing the fandango in Seville, with roses in their hair; in Charleston, the ladies and the gentlemen throw their cigarettes into the hibiscus tubs and flock back into the auditorium; everything as always, no change in the sections, the number of engagements; of one thing they are certain, that they will not puff the smoke off through their nostrils endlessly.

BERTHOLD

With reduced means and far from nature, you live in an urban district which lies deserted Sundays in summertime. You must bring yourself to admit that such Sundays in summertime should grow fewer and fewer, what a drag. On such days, you travel in style, take yourselves to one of the beautiful lakes, overcrowded, but still water and sails and haze: the skin turns red, the wind brushes your flanks, a strange experience, it is the other, Nature - also the tanned long legs of lazy wives in baskets or on stools divert you, fine hours, free and tiring but agreeably so: hours - though the whole, what makes you stop there?

DONATH

Or you stretch yourself at the foot of a terrace,* it is all occupied. The ladies' faces surrender to the night, to the male, to love; the gentlemen's countenance is imposing, their cheeks smooth. The ladies' looks are delicate, sad cowed and sweet against fate. So the nights pass. Devotion, love, one is prepared to suffer on account of a great passion which expires either because nothing lasts or because of an early disappointment.

CILLY

You are just stupid. Talking only of my brown suit, may I still carry the coat or be mindful of the skirt - and then the new muffs, everything else comes automatically, we make no difficulties whatsoever.

ALFRED

To look is sometimes too beautiful, and too short to be able to explain - there lies the distressing dilemma, between glance and hallucination.

BERTHOLD

Or the moon hangs strangely in the sky, rather pale but still big. Above all the streets, its huge oval reminds you of storms, wrinkles, ends and darkened hours. There you might be of some help, bring luck, but then you hurt your own self that strives for intoxication and a certain rapture, for fulfillment and consummation. A word of compassion uttered in a strained way at the wrong moment, you blow it all and the desert is back - this incomprehensible weakness beyond everything, this world of kindness, on the one hand, and on the other, something better to be left alone.
Great Father, say a word.

THE VOICE

What should it be?

DONATH

Or perhaps an autumn evening, fog and something gold-yellow behind, a bridge makes itself scarce and hides its arches. Step back, says a voice. You are by far the perfect casualty - hold your horses, says the other voice, above all, cast your penetrating glance farther on.

EXAMPLE I

Let me sing with you. There is a dance floor there; an affectionate couple, the feet move according to the rules, at the waist they are wrapped round each other, above, already interbreeding; he sings with the text in her mouth, the mouth has white teeth, and all this time, he lets her dance under his arms to the last - that is sweeter than orgasm.

EXAMPLE III

If that is not sensual -

BERTHOLD

Example I, what is your occupation?

31

EXAMPLE I

Fruiterer - sour grapes and horse droppings.

THE VOICE

The great web - it should be so.

PART TWO:

THE SUNDAY NEWSPAPER

EMIL

Great Father, I'm bringing you a Sunday paper. The Lord's day
is disposed of when you are through with the paper; it deliv-
ers man, beast and greens, it contains all your works. These
Sunday papers are enormous! They inform you about the great
light and the little, the fog that dampens the land, water in
Ethiopia and water in Hidaka; they replace the tree of life
and the tree of knowledge, and do justice to the seven days
of the Creation on only thirty-six pages.
We need to look up the table of contents if we want to read
further; the will to form is not regenerated by productivity,
it needs substance.*For many years, the fine artist led an
even and unconcerned life, all quiet there, and would create
out of his own inner resources. But now, only shocks could
lead him on, sensations, broad knowledge and press reports -
here they are grandly presented, instructive and helpful
- he takes root in this mine of information, enriches himself
on detail and holds sway over its features.
Let us start with page one. Thereby one comes to wonder
whether man has on purpose been conceived so, that everything
about him should be wrong: he cannot prevent wars, he cannot
set up any righteous social order, and whenever he takes to
thinking, it is likely to be tragic.

CILLY

Page one without me. Can't you start with the woman's world?
Last Sunday, there was something with Charlotte Buff*in it,
married to a civil servant, yet her grave was left unattended,
very sad, don't you have anything of that sort?

EMIL

Fashionable shades in Paris in 1792: puce-colour, fly-rump
colour, the colour of Parisian mud; you'll get it all, Cilly,
keep quiet. So page one. Once again banknotes of various
denominations are exchanged and fluctuating quotas hold
plenary meetings. That must be so, indeed. The importance
of fixed margins is beyond any doubt: history demands it.*

THE VOICE

Emil, I find your attitude quite unbecoming. The masses are
always right, how could people find employment through the
ads if nothing of the kind is published beforehand? Besides,
today's human beings* have a genuine need of meaning and
expressed opinions, as earlier, they had a need of rituals;
the exchange of news is the present-day cosmos of the silvery
planet Earth.

EMIL

Very true, Papa. We turn now to page three, to conventions
and congresses. The theme of the conference is "The Cruelty
in Fairy-Tales." The speaker presented alarming statistics
of the abominations in the fairy-tales collected by the
Grimm brothers, in support of bitter, real experiences of
cruelty and demanded the suppression of the fairy-tales. Mrs
K., the best informed of the modern experts in children's
literature, was able to produce interpretations that cast
light upon the matter from a historical and psychological
perspective. The deep fear of their step mothers and of the
black man that children feel -

CILLY

Do you have any recollection of that? I cannot remember
anything.

EMIL

Keep your mouth shut, then: it's the experts who talk here.
Let's go on: "Professor T. and Doctor Z., two of the partic-
ipating psychologists, referred to the unreal aspect."

CILLY

How's that, unreal? I suspect that someone there wants to
cure something.

EMIL

But there are also happier reports, also more positive com-
munications and brighter hopes - the federal railway company
and the Pen Club are at it, and those two have got real power!
At the head of all, marches Snow-White in all the horror.
Ortega y Gasset too has given his opinion on that matter. Nobody says anything about the Iliad or Heine's "Three Grena-

deers."* On the contrary, the speaker on one of the panels
pointed to the doubtful pedagogical value of the stag's bel-
lows and cautioned against trips into the woods during the
month of October. Applause.

THE VOICE

What about the floral arrangements?

EMIL

Only impatients and creeping forget-me-nots. Raw food was
highly recommended for festive meals, while Rotkäppchen
bubbly and Henkel-brut were forbidden.

THE VOICE

We are here openly facing the question of prophylaxis. Prophylaxis from whom, for whom, against what, from which stand-
point and in which direction. A self-sustaining point of
crisis.

EMIL

But firstly the ads! I love the ads for the common people.

CILLY

We are all common people.

EMIL

For them I need the magnifying glass. "I take it that where I
go a broken clock stands by me" - it peels out of Loewe's,
Loewe's ballads gather a great many in front of it. "Antlers,
roe horns, nose horns, elephant ivories" - the tropics stand
before the door. "Cock-a-doodle-doo - hen and cock are looking for old china, a special kind of china with artistic
blossoms on it -" we don't need to go into salons, commerce
and industry have their word here, too. We are an amazing
nation. Everything that is ellegant comes from abroad, what
is fascinating, from overseas. As a whole, we are no longer
in the lead, but the ads are made up.

DONATH

Already eleven o'clock, and no second breakfast. You don't
need to read to me anymore. All newspapers are alike. Indeed,
one learns everything from newspapers. The feel of action,
the sensation of flight, the lights of Paris and the prefab
houses on the rim of salty deserts; the reconstitution of the
past and the prospects for the year 2000. One gets it all in
no time, it's a large filing cabinet in which all is crammed.

BERTHOLD

Shut! What happens to intercourse is far worse, for sure.
Recounting, laughing, the cigar sticking out, the ladies
fluttering their hands in ellegant gestures - all that may
still work round a small table. But in any other circumstances,
the younger generation cannot communicate with their elders
any longer: there it's impulse, here it's experience, and in
the absence of any material pressure, the effects are quite
different. The man of religion and the child of this world
cannot talk to each other; because the latter does not share
in the gift of faith, his thinking is flat and linear. Mother
and daughter cannot talk to each other, and so the daughter
keeps secret her sensual gratifications and her shame. The
artist and the politician cannot talk to each other: the
latter is modern, while the former is dated. The industrial-
ist talks of refrigerators and the danger of excessive exports
- who listens to that? A gentleman went to Arosa; snow kept
falling from Thursday until Monday: "In all fairness I must
say that it was too much;" whether fair or unfair, why add
ethical expletives? He should have taken into account the
inclemency of the weather if he had intended to venture to
such heights; in short: why introduce this chummyness, when
we already know that we live in a world of opposites - or I
have been invited to some chap who gives "The Black Bottom"
as his address. That sounds like a morass, wild boars and
long, winding trails, at the end of which one is supposed to
to be entertaining; how can he expect that of me, I have no
sandals for that.

ALFRED

Tohuwabohu,* but nobody wants to know about it; quite a large
additional tax assessment, but nobody wants to pay it. Twilight, in the blue drizzle, the evening whitens the hour;
neither owl nor lark, neither bat nor cock. Zigzag. I saw

trees down below, from a hotel window. A lucky incident had led me into that building. A barcarole; tree-top, underneath, the Canadian quince that had been brought over by a captain, a hundred years before; blue waves and stars, and the sudden arrival of the night.I thought of my sins. Which is the yardstick for sins? A Sunday newspaper was lying on my bed-side table, in it I found the words which Goethe* uttered when he was eighty: "Courage is a matter of luck, and I've got that courage!" So courage has nothing to do with affliction, renunciation, ascesis - it is only a matter of luck! But does the old gentleman say what luck is? My strokes of good luck were, to be precise, all coupled with misdeeds: adultery, drunkenness, perfidy, filial hatred, falsehood, double-standards; Hamsun's turn of phrase*comes to mind, too:"There is only one love, that which is stolen" - one of the truest sayings in the history of mankind; would Goethe have recommended it? But does one ever know where one stands with him, what he means: did he mean anything at all? Annoyed I threw the paper on the floor. From hindsight I only knew what I was thinking; as long as I lived, my brains were stretched over a frightfully hard foundation, now it casts superdestructive arrow-heads ; or perhaps someone else besides me suspects how frightfully near dullness substance lies, the ripeness, the spirituality: practically only the misdeed pushes one on.*

THE VOICE

The critical point.

EMIL

Now here is something for you, Cilly, in the 'High Society' column, soul-stirring, it is conveyed in the form of a modern ballad, as the saying goes, this is ambrosia for the artist. I start:
    Little old lady
    in a big red room
    little old lady *
    hums Marion Davies,
    while Hearst, her friend for thirty years,
    in heavy copper coffin guarded by a strong escort,
    and followed by twenty-two limousines,
    arrives at the mausoleum of marble,

softly purr the television cameras.

Little old lady, big red room,
 henna-red, soft red of gladioli, imperial red (purple
                                        molluscs).
Bed-room in the castle at Santa Monica,
Pompadour-style -

Louella, she calls, radio!*
The blues, jitterbug - zigzag!
The cream of the bourgeoisie in the Atlantic room:
Daughters ripe for marriage, and obliterated sex,
Pallazzi on the bays, eiderdowns on couches,
The world divides itself into Monde and Demi-Monde -
I was always of the latter -

Louella, my cocktail - make it stiff!
What should all that be -
humiliated, desperately fought for, doggedly endured -
the procession, the horrid procession that the copper
                        coffin is bringing to an end,
glowing all over, whenever he saw me,
the rich love, too, tremble and know perdition.

Made it stiff - the glass to the silver shaker,
he would remain silent each and every hour
which only the two of us knew -
funny ditties popped in the receiver:
'in breakfast dens life makes up its mind,
'at the beach, in bathing suit, it hails the rock,
'the unexpected is in the habit of happening,
'the exalted does not come to pass -'
those were his stories.

The promenade is over! Only some flagstones,
on the farthest, the glass,
quite stiff, clinks, last rhapsody -
little old lady,
in a big red room. -

CILLY

And do you know how it goes on? The family landed; after ten

days the will was opened, and she was the sole heiress. Six
weeks later she married a handsome, American naval officer.

EMIL

Truly, if that's the case I shouldn't have bothered to put it
in verse so nicely. Great Father, this is a well-calculated
change of life-style.

THE VOICE

What else should it be?

FERDINAND

First, on page five! These papers have something exotic
about them. Take this one! All the worlds which you haven't
seen. Room made of stone as red as the clouds; landscapes in
which nothing stirs, some smoke from a ranch, a bird like an
arrow. The shed skin of a snake, as thin as cellophane, lies
across the road; big stagnant pools in their erratic furrows.
Wild cats, drunk from the juice of nightshade, shriek, wail,
stagger. What are you looking at? At creatures that you never
have been and never will turn into, cannot afford - worlds of
such creatures - intolerable!

EMIL

And abroad, the assault starts at the tropics. West Africa in
the forefront, but also Nigeria. Here, like a commercial ad:
"Nigeria seeks felt hats." Now we can feed ten billion in an
area where until quite recently 800,000 people lived - what an
incoming flood! But who rushes here - perhaps you? Surround-
ings rich in events! New South Wales has had the coldest day
in seventy-nine years: snow in Canberra; short-lived army
rebellion in Honduras? And you? You know the change of the
agenda that readily may omit something. The Indian zoo is offered a fluted salamander as a token of friendship by Japan;
our hope lies in science, one with an eye* infected with
bladder worm can support himself, but you? Let us say it
quietly: you lay it on the line! And where is the line running
to, into the neige d'antan.*

GERHARD

Well, take the newspaper away, it is too spiteful. Failure and incompetence flood the minds, torrents of homesickness and November, torrents from Land's End and Finisterre. Asia, Africa, Honolulu stifle your flame: granite, mountain ranges, expanses of ice, tulip islands pass over you with their brazen existence; you are lost: have you got the physical strength to stretch out your hand to them - have you got the money? Nowadays, I'm training myself in radar thinking,* let me show you.

EXAMPLE V

I am the radar thinker. Here matter is no intruder, I've checked. The man in the window, the trains of thought inside his own home. Out in the street, he assumes the carriage of asserted individuality, but no sooner, he is back in his attic. I'm working out my own causality. I keep my head empty, inside it one must always have some empty room left for images. My equipment works with method: it always shuts itself automatically, sticks itself to the palate, tastes with the tip of the tongue, is its own paprika, plucks the kittens on its own, a lot of things as such, and a pinch of Seculum-Hallo, that is the radar thinker!
Among my rules of conduct: flee remoteness,* flee abundance of detail; after you read all that, you know, the question is back again: has it not happened on purpose, the splitting of the atom, dynamite, insulin, sweet lupin - what then, how is the thing going to get better; but firstly, either something else presumably happened, or secondly, nothing else happened, still, has anything changed in the rules of the world? No, flee remoteness, flee durability, involve yourselves with your inner strengths, gauge, plumb, hoard, but no sooner, back to images. You read the newspaper, that is, you sublimate the type-mould. Bright, clear-cut trees and flowers surge out of the shades - the principle of the Japanese garden - that is what makes my window so alluring to you. You keep yourselves in the shade, you hold back, that is the way of the world.

HERWARTH

Most likely a relation of Example II, retired. With him we don't go any farther either. This pressure cooker is obsolete: Odol, aspirin, pyramidon, how all that prevails over life while so many need it. Unfashionable, this hollow. Our grand-

parents could think radar-wise. It made possible shrewd,
handsome arrangements: syndic, cunning settlements and new
missions; or a nose, throat and ear specialist, daubing the
throat a little and no night calls - salesman for Suchard
chocolate, in high demand, you needed only to pick up the
receiver and make a note of the order; nowadays you must keep
your claws uncovered day and night,subsidize the blackguards,
knock at the doors, spin and turn round,flatter and threaten,
follow up advertisments, wagging around; have you paid attention to the falling pitch in the voice of your bosses at the
end of the day when they leave the office:"anything else?"

ISAAC

All in all, half the Sunday is generally but pretence ridden
by doubt. A heap of notions, theses, ambitions and no answer.
In each Sunday issue you hope to find an answer, an Ave Maria,
a liturgy, but instead, always these signs of punctuation and
nothing behind them. You read the paper from start to finish,
even the small print, and then you step out into the day-
light, and if you want to get hold of something you have to
approach it with your barest soul.
At times I am inclined to think that the Procreator told
himself: they only need five fingers to break out of the
shell; and in essence, he is right: so perhaps we might have
got these five fingers in our inner selves, too, but that's
impossible; this organization has got only wings and fins, the
means of motion in undetermined media. Only the flesh stirs
itself with more self-assurance. But the whole, including
spirit, style, and custom - what is that then?

THE VOICE

What should it be?

ISAAC

Great Father, if man does no longer dare to look up from the
newspaper and keep asking universal questions, if man dares
to ask nothing any more, what is really wrong with the Procreator; in tigers and leopards, for instance, the murderous
streak and bloodthirstiness have been well devised, but inside ourselves many things are not as they should be or could
have been. You know what it means when one's heart is break-

ing. As a rule, you don't give a damn about it, it's someone else's business, whom you destroy, most often a good man,
a believer that accepts everything from you. Naturally, you
might say that to believe is to sin, that man must wrestle
with the most horrible in every situation; but what is the
purpose of all those songs that sound so sweet then, on
the accordion and the guitar - there must be something beyond
the dreadful. One reads all the papers through and through,
keeps subscribing to new ones, but one finds nothing more;
man's got a sack over his head, knocks himself over, turns to
the Procreator, prays to G...

THE VOICE

Leave G.. out of the game. Even if you've worn your rubber-
soles out, still he's no jobbing cobler,for that very reason.

ISAAC

Not that, although one thinks of him time and again. Before
long comes the hour when you must confront the face in the
dark, the big black swan, then the shadows hurl upon you, and
from amid the shadows you can make amends no more,nor can you
atone any longer. You live on in the knowledge and recollec-
tions of others about you - relative, posthumous fame -
should not man live for it, before the shadows descend?

THE VOICE

Get thee to a nunnery, Ophelia!

ALFRED

But, Great Father, fir branches are back again on the pianos,
and kittens, too, all too soon, please read the article on
Advent; the seasons and the Christian holidays chase us round
and round: once more, and once more; but then, Great Father,
what is it then - say a word, a least.

THE VOICE

What should it be?

BERTHOLD

And the record reviews, these hit songs, the haven of Adorno

and the legs of Dolores make them head swim, a battery of
newspaper niceties, unsteady, mellow moods, this year, and
next, but then, Great Father, what then?

THE VOICE (threatening)

What should it be?

KATYA

One is abandoned for the other, well, one is young, the
other old, one trusts each in turn : "Like a god* each one did
I welcome" (Ariadne, Strauss), but when he is gone, one
is left alone and starts reading the weddings section again,
and the wrinkles appear, the restless nights, the menopause
- where is then the holy - where is it then?

THE VOICE (bellowing)

What should then be, who would be yours, destined and be-
trothed, the eyes behind the tears and the hearts to and fro?
Swallow all your heart and your legs once for all and hold
your trap about your tripes, or as the Psalmist sings: my soul
is quiet before God.
What should then be, you already call holy what I only call
silly, your cheap gibberish, panic-ridden with feelings and
the bladder - always quick on the potty! Could you get an idea
what an eon is - but from where should you get the full
notion?
Your intellectual chimpanzees carry on your liquidation
sale - rentiers, whores, landlords, cadgers of free seats
neighing in the gallery when on the stage hearts stop beating
- what should then be; how many nights have the lonely kept
awake, suffering grief without a babble - nothingness, your
nothingness was jangling on for ever in prayer-mills and
shoe-buckles - when I would say to you: in darkness to live*
in darkness to do what we can - **should that be it**?
What am I losing my temper for, after all? I said to you: had
I begotten you? As a whole, that was too personal and mechan-
ical a way of treating the matter, I had not thought of you,
to be sure. As I was going out with your mother, I was thinking of something else, love always made her face so beautiful.
Children are strangers, they must restrain themselves before
their elders, as well as in my presence, when I tell them

45

about procreation.

Here take both your bells, too, that's another intellectual
farce (throws the bells over the screen). I'll smoothe my
beard with something else, I shall watch a garden in summer
and afterwards look at the snow falling, and nothing else.

(All sing out of the newspaper)

A strange, old stream*was running,
a Nile, white at times, blue at others,
and in the end gushed under our skin,
branching into the play of thought and of love.

Many inherit, but few do earn,
old source, still spitting out the new,
our father died a long time ago,
still he had procreated us well and good.

He has vanished in the big forest,
in the dark green bushes,
he has wriggled through the brushwood,
earnest and manly, and we sing his praise.

PART THREE:

MELANCHOLY AND NEON LIGHTS

EXAMPLE I

Two months later. By now we certainly are all mature, both morally and spiritually. I said to her: you should remain with your new friend, the one you've cheated me with, a greengrocer selling cucumbers. I was shouting, my voice resounded so strangely; I get out of the tub straight away, she said. I knew it. Take out your denture, I was shrieking, and show the good man that you have only two teeth left in the upper jaw. I used to love you in spite of it, I am not so sure about him. That she took amiss. I stopped by my lady-friend, a famous personality, a VIP, my safer haven out of which I attempt my projection, zigzag. In New Cologne there is a bar equipped with desk telephones and a telephone booth in the saloon; today I'm straggling in that direction.

CHORUS

That is the will to live, tremendous.

EXAMPLE IV

The rent increase has been ruled out, but I'm not giving them any hot water. I've been saving the water money for some six years, already. By the way, none of the Dussels has noticed, otherwise, naturally, there might be good reason for legal action. My new house in Düsseldorf is rather small: I have to lay three carpets one upon the other, but nobody there knows what I've got; there are stinkers and quarrelsome people there, too, the world teems with tenants. I've ordered the caretaker not to give anything away; he must use chicanery until they piss fuel oil: no lift, no window panes, no tiles for the roof - ridiculous, this modern civilization, think of it: the dwellings for such parasites are even furnished with kennels! Good-bye, no offence meant.

CHORUS

That is the sense of acquisition that builds up nation-states.

EXAMPLE II

Meanwhile I allowed myself another dozen sessions of ultrasound, one must keep up with the times.

CHORUS

That is life's twilight, under the protection of social welfare and its provisions.

EXAMPLE III

The police behaved great: remained in the first room until we removed the equipment, whips, ropes, handcuffs. At the end, they said: Madam, your flat has only three rooms, and you have declared five chicks as your tenants: where do the five ladies dream after the day's toil and trouble? In the seventh heaven, I said, and the gentlemen laughed. It's the women's associations that are behind all this sensuality campaign. On their part, the inspectors were officials on their best behaviour.

CHORUS

That is love in all its varieties,about which a chorus in one of Aeschilus' plays* has already said:'Oh, Eros, you win no battles.'

CHORUS LEADER

These have been a few examples, but are they beautiful? Have they been given by profound people? Who is a profound human being? Was Socrates profound? He misled the youth about the essence of the state, but died unruffled. Alexander, Muhammad, Eisenhower - is the elemental profound or the sublime, is the good profound or the misdeed? Were there only martyrs and penitents, then where would we stop? And when should we all be silent? No more great father to give us advice!
'So sink, then, man can also say, arise'(Faust) - what does that mean now? Obviously, there are both negative and positive charges. Somewhere, something bursts into flame and somewhere else, something else dies out, somewhere a nova,and somewhere else another grain of sand joins the ashes of the world. Where do we stand, at which point of the fauna, through what flora does our step forces its way? Much is said about that: it is a dream of autumn, the roses bend over their glass: empty; a last rill on the decorated wall,the gardens whisper,

brown and lilac, penetrating the flat, distant lands.

Thus the roses sink, but out of Type E2 dwellings in residential blocks on piers, with motor-drives, swimming pools, restaurants and even a hotel for family guests, man would raise his eyes past the new elders. Why do we keep asking: what then? We all must come to an end.One more word about our geographical position. It might be said that we are big in our local patriotism, native beggars, battering rams - nay, it's the prevailing impression in all Europe. A diplomat from the most safeguarded land on earth, no German, internationally known through the higher offices which he had held, writes the following, by way of an opinion:'The clearest signs of the full and catastrophic transformation of the era in its last stage were already there, the stage in which suddenly all the names, all the words lose their meanings, the symbols which the spirit had erected in architecture and expressed in musical works have ceased to be true, everything lies, everything fades, only to become illegible and then disappear entirely."Monstrous words!It is a diplomat who is taking the soundings here! One who comes from an old-fashioned, distinguished family, the best of Europe as far as social rank and the spaciousness of golf manners go. He pronounces himself in detail about the last stage of our era. No, we do not suffer from local hybris, we are no super-polis, it is the Continent, which is omitted, that has its yoke broken and its ropes torn to shreds.

So all is confusion, blood, spittle, tears, sperm, who is to say what is right and what is important? We bend to all the four cardinal points, the compass card is far too small. The great web, the sacred in all. Ever to take one's fate into one's hands, grief and light, melancholy and neon-lighting, arrogance, churlishness, spoliation, and then the higher things: the cupful of hemlock and the thorns on the cross. Before whom should we still go down on our knees? The old man has left us in the lurch, our condition is bitter. Time and again to take charge of one's fate - yours, Examples and Narrator, before what could we still fall on our knees? At the most, I presume, before his strange words:"We live in darkness, in darkness we do what we can" - but how are we to interpret that?

NOTES

All the notes are the American editor's and are listed in paginal order. They are both explanatory and meant to place the play in the wider context of Gottfried Benn's overall literary work.

Page 16   **Dedicated to my wife.** In the present play, Benn resumes the dialogue between generations which he started in THREE OLD MEN (1949), though in a different form, and with particular people in mind, as the dedication points to. They are the younger generation to which his third wife, Ilse, and his daughter, Nele, belong. In a letter of 18 March, 1952, accompanying a copy of the play and addressed to the latter, Benn describes the play as something new, dreadful about love.... Nonetheless, more of a realist than he would have ever admitted, Benn does not draw an unsurpassable line between the two generations, namely those who had lived through two world wars, on the one side, and those born between those wars, on the other. Although the Great Father's ideas and reactions remind one of Benn's own, his life experience embraces all the members of the cast, so to speak. The dialogue is a back-and-forth movement through that realm of experiences, associations, contradictions, expectations and disappointments. There is no false modesty in his words about the play in the letter addressed to Dr. Oelze at the time of its publication:"It is G.B.'s meddling with pure culture: cynical and melancholic..."(12 March, 1952). He had expected the publication of the play to increase the hostility shown to him by various circles, as he wrote to Ernst Junger on 16 March, 1952. Eventually THE VOICE proved a success with the wider audiences through its radio-broadcasting, not in the least because it was addressing the present without obliterating the past, but looking for the humanly eternal that secures the transition from one to the other.

Page 18   **The programme reads.** Alfred is referring to a theatre programme with its usual summary of the play's plot: a discussion between two generations. It is also an indirect reference to the Shakespearean metaphor of the world as a stage and of people as actors in AS YOU LIKE IT. Berthold is a lagger, he seems not very deft at defining his part and so overcoming the incoherence of his existence. As it would be seen below only the Examples do not worry about the meaning of their lives: they belong to the older

52

generation.

Page 19   **one should crawl into the gutter**. In Benn's inventory of
metaphors, the gutter is the last stage in the lives of non-
conformists and people of genius alike. See, for instance,
his essay "Artists and Old Age" (PV, p.198).

Page 20   **Puerperal fever**. Medical terms and concepts are a trade-
mark of Benn's creative writing, both in verse and prose,
often associated with his protagonist, Dr. Werff Rönne.
Here they are scattered throughout the play. Benn is almost
a classical example of an author who expands the belle-
tristic universe by making extensive use of knowledge
acquired in the practice of an altogether different profession.

roundness of the finale. While Benn was indeed a practising
physician, he remained only an amateur musician throughout
his life. The closest he got involved with it was as the
writer of the text for Paul Hindemith's oratorio, THE
PERPETUAL. Nevertheless, as this metaphor shows, Benn used
musical images in all his writings with the same purpose
and effect as he did medical terms, though less extensive-
ly. Their employment in places where one expects them
the least successfully opens new perspectives upon otherwise routine aspects of everyday life. In this way, the
handbells which Alfred places behind the screen are lent a
new meaning, different from but not altogether excluding
that of the handbells used ritually in the Roman-Catholic
mass.

as the Tao puts it. In Benn's vocabulary "Tao" stands for
the wisdom of sublimated experience and sound, enduring
tradition. He uses it as a term of contrast and as a yardstick by which he measures the acts and gestures of his
contemporaries in the Western world, and finds them wanting. See also the play THREE OLD MEN, the First Dialogue
(PV, p.165).

Faces, faces. The metaphor of the vacuous being whose lack
of personality is dissimulated behind its carefully and
pedantically worn apparel, is one of Benn's tools to
depict some of the post-WWII human characters. See, for
instance, the 1950 poem "Fragments":"...This is the
human being of today,/inside a vacuum,/the continuity in
his personality/is guaranteed by his garments,/which if
the cloth is good, may last ten years" (PEP, p. 245).

teeth out. This list of extirpated organs brings to mind
one of Benn's early poems, "Appendectomy"(1912), though
with a difference: while in the earlier poem, surgical

intervention had as purpose to save lives, nowadays, its
main reason is prophilaxis.

Page 21   **thieves of scrap metal.** In post-WWII Berlin, which was a
heap of ruins, scavenging became a lucrative occupation.
Besides, the acute shortage of sanitary equipment led to
all kinds of shady ways to meet local demands, as well as
those beyond the city's boundaries.

Page 22   **seven years with Calypso.** A literal translation of the
phrase is "seven years Calypso", which indeed is more
ambiguous. As calypso also means a particular kind of
satirical ballad, improvised in the Caribbeans,accompanied
by rhythmic movements, the phrase may also mean that he,
Odysseus had been dillydallying for seven years.In Part II
of the play, Emil would produce a specimen of calypso
about Marion Davies and Hearst, the newspaper magnate.

I run a salon. Benn had acquired a professional knowledge
of brothels during the German occupation of Brussels in
WWI, when as a military phyisician, he was assigned to one
them, reserved exclusively for the occupation army. Thirty
years later, this time in occupied Berlin, he resumed his
medical practice as a specialist in venereal diseases, with
a clientele made up both of occupiers and occupied.

Page 23   **in the style of Dehmel.** Richard Dehmel (1863-1920) German
poet and writer, widely popular before WWI, author of a
collection of poems, entitled REDEMPTIONS, had also written
a book for children in cooperation with his first wife.

Page 24   **observations, comparisons.** Benn is never sparing of the
triviality and futility of most that has been passing for
institutional scientific research. His scathing attitude
finds expression early in his literary career, as for instance, in his conversation piece of 1914, ITHACA.

Page 25   **Now we want to sing the arias.** Since an aria is meant
to be sung by one person alone, what follows is neither a
trio nor a quartet, but the unconnected, lyrical rendition
of snippets of their individual sentimental experiences
by each character in turn, without any one of them paying
heed to what the others are saying.

Page 26   **Early in the morning.** Variations in the light of day,
flowers on window sills or in gardens, music that comes
out of windows, balconies that look out over tree tops,
gardens and parks, all belong to Benn's stock-in-trade
as a poet, alongside houses and their attics that symbol-
ize both refuges and observatories for the lonesome and
the forlorn. See also his 1929 essay "Primal Vision"(PV,
pp.29-38) and such poems as ''Garden and Nights", ·"Frag-

ments' and "Many Autumns"(P, p.55, PEP, pp.245, 253, re-
spectively).

Page 27   **at the foot of a terrace**. The crowded terrace cafés and
           restaurants are other of Benn's favourite images.See also
           his poems "Many Autumns" and "Fifty-Fifty" (PEP, pp.253,
           263).

Page 31   **it needs substance**. Benn takes this opportunity to reassert
           the need of substance in any creative endeavour, an
           issue which he had raised as early as 1931 ("The New Lit-
           erary Season", PV, pp.45-55), if not earlier. Here, he
           briefly defines the difference between past and present
           artists, which in his opinion, rests in the nature of the
           substance they use and in the nature of their relationship
           to society.

           Thereby one comes to wonder. Benn had already pondered
           extensively upon the human being and its purpose, during
           the last years of WWII. Those thoughts were collected and
           printed in 1949, under the general title of WORLD OF EX-
           PRESSION. See, in particular, the fragment "Pessimism"(PV,
           pp.105-109).

           something with Charlotte Buff. It was to Charlotte Buff
           (1753-1828) and to her fiancé that Goethe dedicated his
           first major book, THE SUFFERINGS OF YOUNG WERTHER. In old
           age, she paid Goethe a visit at Weimar, event that became
           the subject-matter of a novel by Thomas Mann, LOTTE AT
           WEIMAR. Goethe had met them at Wetzlar, in his student
           years, and became a great admirer of Charlotte.

           history demands it.Benn attaches more than one meaning to
           the term "history" in his writings. Here, for instance,
           it is a human device used to justify acts or decisions
           of a dubious character. Another meaning is that of an
           inescapable phenomenon, not unlike fate. In his "Answer
           to the Literary Emigrants"(1933), history is a construc-
           tive, form-and-image-laden moving principle, imbued
           with the tragic. Whereas, in the "Way of an Intellectual-
           ist"(1934), history is conceived as a stratified accumu-
           lation of events that might serve as evidence of the
           course followed by evolution. Still, in other instances,
           history is a mere record of trivial events or a slow-
           running, murky and meandering river(THE PTOLOMEAN, 1949).

Page 32   **today's human beings**. The need of meaning and expressed
           opinions is, according to Benn, a characteristic trait of
           our era of unreflecting minds and broken communication
           not only between generations but also social categories
           of people.

Heine's "Three Grenadiers". Heinrich Heine (1797-1856) German poet and author of Jewish descent. The reference to his
ballad is faulty. Actually there are only two grenadiers
in it. This is not an error on Benn's part, but an irony,
a stylistic device by which Benn reveals Emil's and the
other characters' pretence and superficial education.
In passing it may be said that all the references to and
quotations from various authors throughout the play are in-
correct whenever they are not imaginary. There is one
exception, though, namely the quotation from the libretto
of Richard Strauss' opera ARIADNE ON NAXOS, farther in the
text.

Page 34   **Tohuwabohu.** It is a Hebrew biblical word, meaning chaos,
which had been taken over by Martin Luther (1483-1546)
and used in his German translation of the Bible. Benn ap-
propriated it and made it part of his everyday vocabulary.
See, for instance, his letter of 27th December, 1950 to
Dr. F.V. Oelze.

Page 35   **the words which Goethe.** Johann Wolfgang von Goethe (1749-
1832),German poet, author, statesman and scientist,exerted
a deep and lasting influence upon Benn, through his works,
as the last outstanding representative of a world in
equilibrium. Goethe's MAXIMS AND REFLEXIONS became a perma-
nent source of meditation for Benn himself.

Hamsun's turn of phrase. Among modern European writers, the
Norwegian Knut Hamsun (1859-1952) had a special place in
Benn's pantheon. He considered the latter's novel THE VIL-
LAGE SEGELFLOSS one of the few books worth having. After
WWII, Benn waxed enthusiastic over Hamsun's postwar diary,
ON OVERGROWN PATHS, published in a German translation in
1949.

practically only the misdeed. The anarchical nihilism in
which artists create is a topic discussed by Benn time and
again. See, for instance, his 1930 essays "Genius and
Health"(Genie und Gesundheit) and "The Question of Genius",
his poem "Pictures" (1943) and last but not least, his
lecture of 1954, "Artists and Old Age."

Little old lady. The first three lines of Emil's ballad
are in English in the original and reappear as a sort of
refrain farther on. The event so sung is the death and
funeral of the American newspaper magnate William Randolph
Hearst (1863-1951). Marion Davies, an irresistible comic
actress, had been Hearst's mistress for decades.

Page 36   **Louella, she calls, radio !** Louella Parsons had been
Hearst's gossip columnist and chief power-broker in Holly-

wood.

Page 37   **one with an eye.** The idea that there are people in this
world, who despite serious physical disabilities, have the
will to make a living by their own resources and even keep
a family with dignity is of a much earlier date. Thus one
comes across it in Benn's 1933 essay "Answer to the Literary Emigrants"(PV, p.47-48). It is such perseverence
against all odds which verges on the miraculous that makes
Gottfried Benn not despair of mankind.

neige d'antan. In French in the original text. A poem of
1934, "Yesteryear"(Einst) contains a similar image of a
track in the snow, which one wonders where it peters out.
This time, however, Benn provides an answer, though as
ambiguous.

Page 38   **in radar thinking.** In 1949 Benn completed an essay entitled
"The Radar Thinker"(Der Radardenker) that was published
only posthumously. Excerpts from it, though, were included
in his memoirs DOPPLELEBEN (Double Life) of 1950 and in
his article "Problems of Lyricism" (1951). In the original
essay, the modern, post WWII frame of mind is outlined with
its unselective receptivity to everything that crosses its
path, so to speak. It lacks any capacity of introspection,
as well as of in-depth analysis and systematic synthe-
sis. Here, however, we are presented with a caricature
of the original type: the Radar Thinker is turned into a
ventriloquistic automaton, deprived of any initiative, and
implicitly, of any will of his own.

flee remoteness. In the chapter "Future and Present"(PV,
p.170) of DOPPLELEBEN, Benn defines form in terms quite
contrary to the advice given here by the Radar Thinker.
There he writes: 'in form is distance, is duration'. In
other words, by his opposition to creative thinking, the
Radar Thinker in the play is made to represent the nihil-
istic vein that lies at the core of conformism.

Page 41   **"Like a god."** The words are Zerbinetta's who is trying to
console Ariadne, abandoned on her isle. See the libretto
of ARIADNE ON NAXOS, opera in one act with a prelude by
Hugo von Hofmannsthal(1874-1929), with music by Richard
Strauss(1864-1949), English translation by Alfred Kalish,
New York, 1958, p.35.

in darkness to live. The idea of acting and living in darkness had been expressed by Benn before, as for instance,
in his essay "Artists and Old Age"(PV, pp.183-208) and
the dialogue THREE OLD MEN (PV, pp.165-174). In the play,
Alfred has already uttered it in his own way (Part One, p.

23):"we always fumble, with a sack pulled down over the eyes and grope along, at best."

A strange, old stream. The Nile has been Benn's favourite metaphor for fluidity, for continuation in change and the subterranean motive forces and hence of history, since early in his literary career. Thus in his 1916 piece "The Birthday," one reads about a "green Nile of the night...". (See also PEP, p.12.)

Page 45 **In one of Aeschilus' plays.** Benn knew and liked Aeschilus' theatre, and most of all his PROMETHEUS. Eventually, he came to see in the latter's EUMENIDS a play as relevant to the modern times.